Joe Schuster

JACKIE ROBINSON

Joe Schuster's short fiction has appeared in *The Kenyon Review*, *The Iowa Review*, and *The Missouri Review*, among others, and his articles have been published in *USA Today*, *St. Louis Post Dispatch*, and the revered, retired *Sport*. *The New York Times Book Review* describes his novel *The Might Have Been* as a "meticulously peopled tale of opportunities lost." *Publishers Weekly* says "Schuster examines, without succumbing to sentiment or an easy resolution, the cost of chasing a dream."

Jackie Robinson is Joe's second book in the Gemma Open Door Series, following the success of *One Season in the Sun*.

First published by GemmaMedia in 2018.

GemmaMedia
230 Commercial Street
Boston, MA 02109 USA

www.gemmamedia.com

Printed in the United States of America

978-1-936846-71-9

Library of Congress Cataloging-in-Publication Data

Names: Schuster, Joseph M., author.
Title: Jackie Robinson / Joe Schuster.
Description: Boston MA : GemmaMedia, 2018. | Series: Gemma open door
Identifiers: LCCN 2018040591 | ISBN 9781936846719
Subjects: LCSH: Robinson, Jackie, 1919-1972. | Baseball players--United States--Biography. | African American baseball players--Biography.
Classification: LCC GV865.R6 S354 2018 | DDC 796.357092 [B] --dc23
LC record available at https://lccn.loc.gov/2018040591

Cover by Laura Shaw Design
Cover image: Bettman/Getty Images.

Gemma's Open Doors provide fresh stories, new ideas, and essential resources for young people and adults as they embrace the power of reading and the written word.

Brian Bouldrey
Series Editor

GEMMA

Open Door

For Kathy and my family,
especially Joe V and Mila

1.

Against the Klan

Jackie Robinson was in a fight with the Ku Klux Klan almost three months before his best baseball season ever. The Klan was angry because Jackie's team, the Brooklyn Dodgers, agreed to play three exhibition games in Georgia against the Atlanta Crackers.

Klan leader Samuel Green said Jackie and his teammate Roy Campanella could not play in the games because they were African Americans. He said it was illegal for black players and white players to appear on the field together in Georgia. Green said he would make sure that Jackie and Campanella were not in the games.

This kind of reaction to Jackie was not new to him during his career. He broke baseball's color line when the Dodgers signed him to a contract three years before. The color line kept all but white ballplayers from playing in the major leagues for many years.

After they signed Jackie, the Dodgers sent him to play for their minor league team in Montreal in 1946 to teach him how to compete in professional baseball. They made this decision because there was less bias against black people in Canada than in the United States. But the Montreal Royals held spring training in Florida. There, Jackie faced great prejudice.

On his trip to Florida from his home in California with his wife, Rachel, he had to change planes in New Orleans. There the Robinsons saw the effect of Jim Crow laws that states in the American South enforced. Jim Crow was a character created by a white singer more than 100 years before Jackie joined the Dodgers. The singer painted his face black and made fun of the language and songs of slaves to entertain white audiences. After the United States outlawed slavery, some states passed laws to keep African Americans as second-class citizens. They named those laws after Jim Crow.

Once the Robinsons were in the South, they were not allowed to eat in the airport coffee shop. They saw signs for whites-only bathrooms and drinking fountains. The airline sold too many tickets for their flight to Florida and gave the Robinsons' seats to white passengers. Jackie took a sixteen hour bus ride for the last part of his trip. Because of Jim Crow laws, the Robinsons sat in uncomfortable seats at the back of the bus even though there were comfortable empty seats in the white section.

When Jackie arrived at spring training, he could not stay in the nice hotel with his white teammates. He boarded with black families in the city. He could not change into his uniform in the team clubhouse with the other players. Instead, he changed at home.

The bias against Jackie even affected him on the field. When it was time for the Royals' first exhibition game in Jacksonville that spring, the city said that "Negroes and whites cannot compete against each other on a city-owned playground." His team canceled the game. When they tried to play another one, the city canceled it. Other cities in Florida decided to keep the team from playing games if Jackie was on the field.

Even though he faced this bias Jackie had a good season with Montreal. He was the best hitter in the league. The next year, the Dodgers decided that he was good enough to play in the major leagues. The team trained in Cuba and Panama, where they were safe from Jim Crow laws. In 1948, they trained in the Dominican Republic for the same reason. Then the team bought land in

Vero Beach, Florida, so that the team could train and play exhibition games but not have to follow most Jim Crow laws.

Because other major league teams trained in Florida cities that still opposed black players competing with white players, the Dodgers played most of their exhibition games in other states.

By 1949, Jackie and the Dodgers were even more tired of the effect of Jim Crow laws. In January, the team announced their plan to play exhibition games in Florida and other states in the American South. They said that Jackie and Campanella would play in those games. If any city or state tried to prevent them, they would cancel the games. They said this meant the city and state would lose out on the money those games might bring them.

Almost right away, cities in Florida and North Carolina said they would let them play. In Georgia it was a different story, especially in Atlanta.

Atlanta was the home base of the Ku Klux Klan, then and now one of the most active groups in the world who oppose rights for people who are not white. Georgia governor Eugene Talmadge had campaigned for his office by calling for racial segregation.

The stage was set for an important fight about race in baseball and America.

2.

A Hard Early Life

Jackie Robinson was born on January 31, 1919, in a small town in Georgia about 200 miles south of Atlanta. He had three older brothers and a sister. Like many African Americans of his time, he was the grandson of slaves. Even though the American Civil War ended slavery more than fifty years before, when Jackie was a baby his family lived in what he called a kind of slavery. His father, who could not read or write, worked on a plantation for about three dollars a week. That equals seventy-five dollars a week by today's standards. Not long after Jackie was born his father left. Jackie never saw him again.

Jackie later wrote a book about his life, titled *I Never Had It Made*. In it, he said that the man who owned the plantation blamed Jackie's mother for his father not working for him anymore. He told her she had to leave. She decided she no longer wanted to live in the South. She moved the family to California. They settled in Pasadena. There, they were still very poor. Jackie's mother earned a little money cleaning houses but it was often not enough. In his book, Jackie says that on some days the family ate only because his mother brought home leftover food from the people she worked for. In an article he wrote for the *Washington Post*, he said, "We would get to school so hungry we could hardly stand up." To help his family, Jackie worked to earn extra money. He delivered newspapers, mowed lawns, sold hot dogs at a football stadium, and worked other odd jobs.

Poverty was not the only hardship he endured as a boy. Even though the family was no longer in the South, they still faced bias because of their race. The Robinsons lived in a neighborhood made up mostly of white families. Some of them shouted an ugly name at Jackie and his siblings that referred to his race. Some called the police with silly complaints. Once it was because they said Jackie's brother's roller skates made too much noise on the sidewalk. One day, someone burned a cross on their lawn. Burning a cross is something the Ku Klux Klan does to frighten black people. None of these things worked to force Jackie's mother to move, and the family stayed in the neighborhood.

What saved Jackie's life was sports, especially after he got to high school. His interest partly came from his older brother Mack, who was a track-and-field champion. Mack was good enough that he won the silver medal in the 200-meter dash at the 1936 Olympics. Years later, Jackie wrote in the *Washington Post* article, "My brother Mack had more to do with my athletic career than any one else. He'll always be a real hero with me. I remember going to track meets with him and watching him run and listening to the crowd yell."

Those cheers for his brother were important for Jackie.

He wrote, "Without him and his encouragement I don't think there ever would have been a Jackie Robinson, baseball player."

Almost from the moment he started high school, Jackie had his own athletic success. He starred on his school's football, baseball, and basketball teams and won tennis championships. He was so good and so fast, one newspaper called him black lightning. In college, he became even better. He first went to Pasadena Junior College, where he played football, basketball, and baseball and competed in track. In football, he was the quarterback. The *Los Angeles Times* said he was the "most brilliant ball carrier ever developed" in the area. Sometimes 50,000 people came to one of his team's games. The *Los Angeles Times* said that ninety-nine percent of those people were there because they wanted to see Jackie play. In track, he set the school record in the long jump. In baseball, he was the Southern California junior college most valuable player.

Because of his success, when he decided to move on to a university, the *Los Angeles Times* said he was the "juiciest plum of the 1939 crop of college-bound athletes." He chose the

University of California, Los Angeles (UCLA) because he wanted to stay near his home.

He was just as successful at the university as he was in high school and junior college. In his two years of football there he led all college players in the country in punt return average. In basketball, he led the conference in scoring in 1939 and 1940. In track, he won the national college broad jump championship. Many predicted he would win the gold medal in that event in the 1940 Olympics. Sadly, the games were canceled when World War II spread through Europe.

Jackie left UCLA early in 1941 and played professional football in Hawaii and California before joining the army as a lieutenant after the United States entered the war. There, he ran into more examples of racism.

Before joining the army, he had a weak ankle because it broke twice while playing football. In the army, he hurt it again in training. The doctors found he had bone spurs and arthritis and sent him to therapy. One day, riding a bus to the hospital for treatment, he sat in the middle of the bus instead of the back where black people were supposed to sit. He sat beside the wife of a friend. She was black but light-skinned. The bus driver ordered Jackie to move to the back of the bus. He accused Jackie of speaking to a white woman, something many thought black men should not do.

The bus driver reported Jackie to the military police. They arrested him and brought him to an officer for questioning. The officer decided that Jackie was disrespectful. Jackie said he was not and that the officer had treated him badly because he was African American. The army put him on trial. In the end, Jackie was found not guilty. Soon after, the army discharged him, saying that his bad ankle meant he was not healthy enough to serve.

His discharge meant that he was not sent with his unit to Europe to fight in the war. Instead, he found himself at the center of a different kind of conflict.

This one was about civil rights.

The stage where it took place was professional baseball.

3.

The Color Line

The first time Jackie Robinson played against major league players was in 1938. He was nineteen and part of a Pasadena amateur all-star team. The Chicago White Sox had their spring training in Pasadena. One day in March the White Sox and the amateur all-star team played an exhibition game to raise money for the city's recreation department. Jackie played shortstop for the all-stars.

That day the White Sox won the game 3–2 but Jackie played well. His team had only six hits but Jackie had two of them. He stole a base and made a great defensive play. On the play, the White Sox batter was Luke Appling. He would later be voted into the Hall of Fame as one of the greatest players in history. The White Sox had a runner on first and Appling drove a ball to the outfield that looked as if it would drop for a hit. But Jackie dove for it and caught it. He then threw to second base for a double play.

After the game, White Sox manager Jimmy Dykes said, "If that Robinson kid was white, I'd sign him right now. No one in the American League could make plays like that."

That day one of Jackie's teammates signed a professional contract. This was pitcher Burt Barkelew, who had a career in minor league baseball until 1955.

But in 1938, Dykes could not sign Jackie because of the color line.

In the earliest years of major league baseball there were a few black players. In 1879, William Edward White appeared in one game for the Providence Grays of the National League. He batted four times, had one hit, and then never played for the Grays again.

Five years later, brothers Moses Walker and Weldy Walker played for the Toledo Blue Stockings of the American Association. In those days, the American Association was one of two major leagues. It folded in 1891. Today, there are again two major leagues. The older is the National League, which was founded in 1876.

The newer is the American League, which began in 1901. Moses Walker was a catcher who appeared in forty-two games. His brother, who played outfield, was in five games.

Moses Walker shows us what life was like for black athletes in professional baseball during the late 1800s. He played well that year. His final batting average was .263. This was higher than all but two other players on his team. Later, one of the team's pitchers said he was a very good catcher. But he suffered because of his skin color.

So that catchers do not make errors on pitched balls, pitchers and catchers usually give hand signals about the kind of pitch a pitcher will throw. Because Walker was African American, one of his team's pitchers would not do this. This meant Walker had no idea where the ball was going to go. This led to errors.

Some teams said they would refuse to play a game if Walker were on the field. In other cities, fans booed him because he was black.

Things became worse. In September that year Toledo was planning to go to Richmond, Virginia, for games. Some Richmond residents sent a letter to the Toledo manager threatening Walker. The note said that if Walker tried to play, seventy-five men would attack and kill him.

Before the team went there, they took him off the roster. The official reason was that he was too injured to play.

Walker spent a few more years in the minor leagues and then left baseball.

After that, some African Americans played ball in the minor leagues for a few more seasons. But by 1900 white professional teams stopped signing black players to contracts. Until 1946, African Americans could only play baseball in what were called the Negro Leagues.

From around 1900 until just after Jackie Robinson broke the color line, Negro League baseball was popular among African Americans. Many of the teams played in the same cities as white major league teams, like New York, Pittsburgh, and St. Louis. Just as white teams had their stars like the home-run hitting Babe Ruth or pitcher

Dizzy Dean, the Negro Leagues had their popular stars.

One of the most famous was Josh Gibson, a catcher for two teams in Pittsburgh, Pennsylvania, from 1930–1946. Because he hit so many home runs, people called him the black Babe Ruth. Some who thought Gibson was even better said that Ruth was the white Josh Gibson.

Another star was pitcher Satchel Paige. He played Negro League ball from 1926–1947. During his Negro League career, Paige pitched against white major league players and beat them. Gibson never made it to the white major leagues because by the time Jackie broke the color line, he was no longer the great player he had been.

Paige pitched in the major leagues. In 1948, he joined the Cleveland Indians of the American League. He was forty-two and the oldest rookie player ever. That year, he became the first African American to pitch in the World Series. Later, when he was with the St. Louis Browns, he was a major league All-Star from 1952–1953.

As a mark of how good he was, in 1965 when he was fifty-eight, the Kansas City Athletics of the American League signed him to a contract as a publicity stunt. The team was the worst in the league that year and sold few tickets. They announced Paige would be the starting pitcher on September 25. They thought he would draw people to the ballpark. He did. In the four games just before he pitched, only a total of about 6,000 people came to the park. One of those games drew only 690. On the day Paige pitched, there were almost 10,000.

He pitched three innings and gave up only one hit. When he left the game in the fourth inning, the stadium turned off its lights and the 10,000 fans lit matches and sang to him.

In 1971, the Baseball Hall of Fame in Cooperstown decided to make up for the years of bias against African American players. It began inducting great players from the Negro Leagues. Today, there are thirty-five Negro League stars with plaques in the Hall of Fame, including Paige and Gibson.

Other Negro League players who

were younger than those two went on to have long and great careers in the major leagues. Hank Aaron, who played in the major leagues from 1954–1976 and broke Babe Ruth's home run record, played one season in the Negro Leagues. Larry Doby, who was the first African American to play in the American League, was a major leaguer from 1947–1959. Both are in the Hall of Fame for their great playing in the major leagues.

The Negro Leagues were where Jackie Robinson got his start as a professional baseball player.

4.

The Negro Leagues

Jackie was not sure what he wanted to do for work after he left the army in 1944. He decided to try being a high school coach because he loved sports. But he thought it would be difficult to get that job. Then he learned that a Negro League team called the Kansas City Monarchs needed players. He decided to try playing for them for one year to get schools interested in hiring him as a coach.

That was his plan. He would give baseball one year and then leave the game.

It did not turn out that way.

He wrote the Monarchs a letter

saying he wanted to join them. They invited him to try out and he signed a contract for $400 a month. This was a lot of money in that era. Today, it would be equal to more than $5,000 a month.

In his book *I Never Had It Made*, Jackie wrote that the money was good, but the life was hard. One time, he said, the team rode a bus for two days from Kansas City to Philadelphia where they played a doubleheader. They got back on the bus that night to travel to another city for another game. In many cities no hotels would allow the team to stay because the players were black. On many days the players had to sleep on the bus. Many restaurants would not serve them. Jackie wrote, "You were really living when you were able to get a plate of cold cuts. You ate on board the team bus or on the road."

Even though the life was hard, Jackie played well. He ended the year with the highest batting average in the league, .414. His play got the attention of several white major league teams. By that year, there were some in the major leagues who decided it was time for the color line to come down. For example, in 1943 an owner named Bill Veeck tried to buy the National League Philadelphia Phillies. He said he wanted to stock the team with great Negro League stars. But the league was not interested and allowed someone else to buy it.

By 1945, teams decided to start

allowing black players to compete. That April, the Boston Red Sox invited Jackie and two other Negro League players to try out. Even the idea that major league teams considered signing black players was a major event. Newspapers across the country reported on the tryout. Most articles said that Jackie impressed Boston manager Joe Cronin more than the others. But the Red Sox signed no African American players that day. In fact, Boston would be the last major league team to sign an African American player. They would wait until 1959, a dozen years after Jackie broke the color line.

Even though Boston was not interested, Jackie's wait was short for another major league team to go after him. After the news came out about the Red Sox tryout, the Brooklyn Dodgers sent scouts to watch Jackie play for the Monarchs. They came back and told the team's president, Branch Rickey, that Jackie was a great ballplayer.

Rickey and Jackie held a few secret meetings. At one, Rickey shouted at Jackie and called him the same name that Jackie's neighbors had when he was a boy. Rickey told Jackie that if he played major league baseball, he would deal with that kind of abuse often. He said he wanted to see how Jackie reacted. Finally, in October, the Dodgers announced that they signed Jackie to a contract and sent him to play for their Montreal minor league team for 1946.

People called it the great experiment because Jackie's career might affect the course of black players in baseball for many years to come. If he succeeded, it would open the door for more African Americans. If he failed, it might make it harder for others to follow him.

Among Jackie's supporters was the president of the Montreal team, Hector Racine. He pointed to the fact that African Americans had risked their lives during the world war that ended earlier that year. He told a reporter from the *Brooklyn Daily Eagle* newspaper, "Negroes fought alongside whites and shared the foxhole dangers and they should get a fair trial in baseball."

The Dodgers expected they would

face trouble because of signing Jackie. Rickey's son, Branch Rickey, Jr., said he thought Brooklyn might lose some very good players who would not want to be on a team with an African American. Less than two years later, some members of the team said exactly this.

The news received both positive and negative responses.

One Montreal reporter said, "No sports story has ever caught the sports public with such intense interest." On the other hand, the editor of the *Sporting News*, the main newspaper that covered baseball across the country, said he thought that the attention Jackie and the Dodgers got was far beyond the worth of the story. He thought Jackie would never reach the major leagues because he was not good enough.

Some players agreed with him. Pitcher Bob Feller, who later went to the Hall of Fame, said, "He doesn't look like a hitter to me. I don't think he will ever be a good hitter."

Others thought Jackie did not belong because of the color of his skin.

Rogers Hornsby, who is in the Hall of Fame for having the highest batting average in National League history, said that white players should play with white players and that "Negro players should remain as stars in their own leagues."

Dixie Walker, an outfielder for the Dodgers, said it was fine if a Negro played in the major leagues as long as it was not on his team. Later, Walker led a protest by Dodgers players against Jackie.

In the end, these opinions about Jackie signing his contract meant little.

The most important thing was how Jackie played on the field. If he played badly, as some said he would, the experiment would fail.

5.

A Crack in the Color Line

Jackie's first game for Montreal drew great attention. The team played it in Jersey City, New Jersey. Even though the ballpark had 25,000 seats, the owner sold more than 50,000 tickets. Half of the people who bought tickets wanted to have a keepsake from the historical moment but were not in attendance at the game.

Newspapers across the country do not usually cover minor league baseball games as major events. But papers from the East Coast to the West Coast published articles about Jackie's first game. One newspaper in a city

3,000 miles from where the game was played ran a headline that said, "Jackie Robinson, First Negro in Organized Ball, Stuns Crowd with Dazzling First Performance."

Indeed, it was dazzling.

The game showed the range of his ability, from speed to power. Jackie came to bat five times and had four hits. Two of his hits were bunts and he stole two bases. He hit a home run.

When he crossed home plate after hitting it, teammate George Shuba shook his hand. This was a common gesture in baseball. But the photograph of this handshake became instantly famous because it was the first photo of a white man shaking the hand of an African American in a professional baseball game. The photo was so famous that even though Shuba had a short and ordinary baseball career, people remember it today. When he died in 2014, major newspapers in America ran articles about his death and his life. The *New York Times* used the headline, "George Shuba, 89, Dies; Handshake Heralded Racial Tolerance in Baseball."

Jackie's entire season in Montreal was a great one. By the end, his .349 batting average was the highest in the International League. His play helped his team win the International League championship by a wide margin. Their record was 100 wins and fifty-four losses. The second place team won only eighty-one and lost seventy-two.

After the regular season ended,

Jackie's team faced the American Association champion, the Louisville Colonels, in the Little World Series. Like the World Series that major league teams play, it was best of seven. This meant the first team to win four games was the victor. In the Little World Series, the top teams from two Triple-A minor leagues (the International League and the American Association) met to determine what they called the minor league world champion.

Jackie played well in the series. He batted .400 and scored the run that won the final game. After it was over and his team won four games to two, fans and newspaper writers said that Jackie was the chief reason Montreal took the championship. After the last out of the last game and Montreal left the field, fans cheered for Jackie until he came back onto the field. Several men lifted him onto their shoulders and carried him around the baseball diamond in a parade. Men clapped his back in celebration. Some women kissed him. Some fans pulled at his shirt so hard, it came off.

After he left the field for good, Jackie found several thousand more excited fans outside the stadium, waiting for him. He dashed through the crowd to get to the car that would take him away. In his autobiography, he wrote that a sportswriter joked, "It was probably the only day in history that a black man ran from a white mob with love instead of lynching on its mind."

With the season a success, Jackie had conquered one level of baseball.

The next year, he would try to conquer another.

The highest level.

6.

Jackie Changes Baseball

When a player does as well as Jackie in Triple-A, people assume he will have a chance for the major leagues the next year. However, Jackie faced many challenges that no other player of his time dealt with.

The first challenge that Jackie faced was that several members of the Brooklyn Dodgers wrote a petition telling the team they objected to playing for the Dodgers if they had a black teammate. When the petition failed, one of them sent a letter to Branch Rickey saying, "I would like to be traded as soon as possible .... For reasons I do not care to go in to, I feel my decision is best for all."

The player was Dixie Walker, who earlier said he was fine with an African American playing for a major league team if he was not with Walker's team.

As the season went on, Walker came to change his mind.

The Dodgers decided that they would put Jackie on their major league roster for 1947. To have an idea of what this meant in that day you have to know that major league teams usually carry twenty-five players. There were sixteen big league teams then. This meant there were 400 major league players.

Three hundred and ninety-nine of them were white.

One was black.

Jackie played his first game on April 15 as the Dodgers' first baseman in a packed ballpark. He later wrote about a memory of that day.

"I remember standing alone at first base—the only black man on the field. I had to fight hard against loneliness, abuse[,] and the knowledge that any mistake I made would be magnified because I was the only black man out there."

He did not get any hits that day. But he did get his first major league hit in the second game. The rest of his first week in the major leagues went well. In his first six games, he had nine hits. He began getting fan letters from around the country. People wrote that they backed him in his effort to succeed. He received hundreds of letters asking him to attend public dinners and events.

Then his year took a dark turn.

In a game against the Philadelphia Phillies, the other players constantly shouted curses at him. They called him the most common slur for African Americans. They told him he should go back to the jungle. They shouted, "Why don't you go back to the cotton fields where you belong."

Their curses got to Jackie. When Branch Rickey signed him to his contract the two men agreed that Jackie would face hatred because of his race. They agreed, however, that if the great experiment was to change baseball, Jackie could not show anger when he received this hate. They thought that might prove that black players could not stand the pressure.

Even though Jackie did not respond in anger to the Phillies, what they said still upset him. He later wrote, "This day, of all the unpleasant days in my life, brought me nearer to cracking up than I have ever been . . . . I felt tortured."

He went into a slump and remained hitless for five games. His average fell to .225 by the end of April, one of the lowest on the team. When he finally managed to get a hit on May 1, things nearly became worse for him.

In fact, he found himself at the center of a fight that nearly ended the great experiment right after it began.

Starting on May 6, the Dodgers had a series of games on their schedule against the St. Louis Cardinals. The Cardinals won the World Series the year before. They were located in the southernmost city of all the major league teams at that time. In fact, every other major league team that year was located in a state that had fought against the South in the Civil War. Missouri was a border state. This meant that during the war some people in the state fought for the North but some wanted to allow people to own slaves and fought for the South.

Even though the war had been over for more than 80 years, those southern feelings still held firm among many in St. Louis. When the Dodgers first signed Jackie, Branch Rickey, Jr., said that one of the things that could lead to the greatest problems was what he called "a strong hangover from the Civil War."

He was right.

This hangover led several members of the Cardinals to say they would go on strike if Jackie Robinson took the field against them for a game. If that happened and they faced no punishment, other teams might follow their lead. That could force Jackie out of the league.

Instead, the Cardinals owner told Ford Frick, the president of the National League, about the possible strike. Frick sent a stern reply to the Cardinals players. He said, in part:

"If you do this, you will be suspended from the league. You will be outcasts. The National League will go down the line with Robinson. You will find if you go through with your intention that you have been guilty of complete madness."

The Cardinals did not strike. At the same time, Jackie broke out of his slump. He had four hits in the three games against the Cardinals and he went on hitting. In all, he had hits in fourteen straight games. By May 17, his average was up to .299.

Jackie had good and bad stretches for the rest of the season but finished the year with a .297 batting average that ranked the third best on his team. His team won the league championship and a year after he was in the Little World Series he found himself in the Major League World Series playing against the New York Yankees.

Even though the Dodgers lost, Jackie received much praise when the season ended. The *Sporting News*, which earlier said Jackie was not good enough to make the major leagues, voted him the Rookie of the Year, the honor that goes to the best first-year player.

Time magazine put Jackie's picture on the cover of an issue it published in late September. Pointing to the names other teams called him and the strike the St. Louis players almost had, it said Jackie had gone through "the toughest first season any ballplayer had ever faced." Even though that was true, the magazine said, "he had made good as a major leaguer and proved himself as a man."

One of the players who was happy for Jackie receiving recognition was Dixie Walker, who was once against any African American being part of his team. After Jackie won the Rookie of the Year Award, the team honored him on the field. Some of the Dodgers went out to shake his hand. One of them was Walker. He later said he came to respect Jackie because of the way he handled the personal attacks on him.

"I grew up in the South," he later said. "We thought that blacks couldn't take the pressure of playing major league ball. We know now that's the biggest farce as ever was. I'll say one thing for Robinson, he was as out-standing an athlete as I ever saw."

7.

The Klan Cannot Control Him

Jackie Robinson had another strong year in 1948. It was not as good as his first season but it was still not bad. The Dodgers finished in third place and Jackie had a batting average that was a little lower than in his first year, .296. As one positive aspect, Jackie had the best fielding average for National League second basemen (fielding average measures the rate of errors a player makes on defense). In 1948, Jackie made an error on only two percent of his plays.

When the year was over, he was disappointed. "I knew I should have done better," he said later. "I made myself a solemn vow to redeem myself and the Dodgers in 1949."

He asked one of the Dodgers' coaches to help him hit better. The coach was George Sisler, who was already in the Hall of Fame because he was one of the best hitters of all time in baseball.

Sisler told Jackie that when he hit a pitch, he almost always hit toward left field. He told him that if he made a change in how he swung the bat he would hit balls to different parts of the field. This would make it harder for the other teams to catch what he hit and would raise his batting average.

The lessons seemed to work. Jackie hit .470 in exhibition games during spring training. This meant that he had nearly one hit every two times he batted.

But just as Jackie faced difficulties for being African American for his entire life, he soon faced it again. The fact that he was among the best major league players of that year did not protect him from bias.

In his autobiography he wrote, "I thought I had learned the worst there was to learn about racial hatred in America. The year 1949 taught me more."

The main lesson came from the Ku Klux Klan.

The Klan was created after the Civil War. Its purpose was to try to create an all-white society. Some members of the Klan used violence to promote their views. Several times after its creation the US government outlawed the group. But they rose up again and again.

By 1949 a Georgia doctor named Samuel Green led the Klan. Green said that the Klan no longer committed crimes or used violence to get its way. But several times in the late 1940s the group was accused of threatening to kill or harm people.

In 1946, they were accused of saying they planned to kill the Governor of Georgia because he wanted to investigate the Klan's illegal actions. Klan members were arrested that year for killing a black cab driver and for beating a black navy veteran.

In 1948 someone accused them of

threatening a high school principal and coach. Green said they did not do that. But some men dressed in Klan robes burned a cross on the coach's lawn while he was out and his pregnant wife was home.

In January 1949 when the news came out that the Dodgers would play a series of games in Atlanta, Green said that he thought these games were illegal because African Americans and whites could not play on the same field.

He told a writer for the *Sporting News*, "God made white people for a purpose and black people for a purpose. Colored players will bring ill will or ill good in the South."

The Dodgers said they would put their best team on the field and that included Jackie and Roy Campanella, who was a rookie catcher that year.

Jackie said, "I will play baseball where my employer, the Brooklyn Dodgers, wants me to play. I hope very much that fans in Atlanta, or all over America, will not allow this objection to cause a cancelation of the game."

Green learned that there was no written state law that made the games illegal.

After this fact came to light, some members of the Georgia legislature introduced a bill to create such a law. Not only would it be illegal for African Americans to play any sports with white athletes, it would be against the law for African American actors and singers to appear on a stage with white singers and actors.

Even though they tried to take this action, it was too late to prevent the Dodgers from playing the Crackers in Atlanta in April.

The game would go ahead.

When Green found this out, he said that he would ask people to sign a pledge saying they would never go to an Atlanta Crackers game ever again if the Crackers allowed Jackie and Campanella to play. He said he had 10,000 people who signed the pledge. He said this would hurt the Crackers in a financial way.

As it turned out, Green lost his battle.

One writer for an Atlanta newspaper said the fate of the games was clear just by looking at the traffic going to the ballpark before the first game. More than an hour before the first pitch, cars packed a main Atlanta street. Almost 16,000 crowded into the park for that first game. This was an unusual number for an exhibition game that carried no weight toward a championship or a league title. Especially in a ballpark that was home to a minor league team.

Jackie said he was nervous the first time he came to bat. Some booed him as he stood at the plate. When he hit a single into the outfield, thousands of black and white fans stood and cheered him, drowning out the boos.

The Brooklyn Dodgers' radio announcer told reporters that the cheering for Jackie, even among white fans, was louder than what he heard in the major league cities where Jackie played. After the games, children—both black and white—waited patiently for Jackie to come out to sign his autograph.

Jackie told reporters, "Believe me, this is the most thrilling experience of my life. It's great to feel that I am playing a part in breaking down the barriers against the people of my race. I was afraid it would never be in my lifetime."

The entire three-game series was a success in every way. Jackie had seven hits in all. The ballpark was crowded every day. Fifty thousand people came to the park for the three games. Twenty-five thousand came just to the Sunday game when the Atlanta Crackers broke the record for its highest-ever attendance. Half of the fans that day were black. The park was so crowded, some had to sit at the edge of the outfield instead of the bleachers. Most were African Americans since African American fans were not allowed to sit in the white sections of the bleachers.

Even though Jackie and Campanella played in the game, there was still a long way to go for equality.

After the series was over, the *Sporting News* said that the success of the games was due mostly to Jackie. They declared that he was another Babe Ruth in the way that he drew fans into a ballpark.

If Samuel Green, the Klan leader, had any response to this, newspapers do not seem to have reported it. Four months later, on August 18, he died while working in his yard.

That same day, Jackie Robinson played baseball in Philadelphia. He had two hits, stole a base, and the Dodgers won the game.

8.

The Greatest Season

In 1949, there were eleven African American players in the major leagues. There were, however, only four teams with African American players. The Dodgers had three of them. Besides Jackie and Campanella they had a pitcher named Don Newcombe. He joined the team in May that year.

The Cleveland Indians had three African American players. Their owner at the time was Bill Veeck, who had tried to buy the Philadelphia Phillies in 1943 and fill it with black players. The other two teams were the St. Louis Browns and the New York Giants.

Because the number of African American players was slowly growing, Jackie and Branch Rickey decided he could be himself.

In his autobiography, Jackie wrote, "There were enough blacks on other teams to ensure that American baseball could never again turn its back on minority competitors."

This meant that Jackie could express his opinion if he did not like the way someone treated him.

In his autobiography, Jackie wrote, "It felt good to be able to breathe freely, to speak out when I wanted to."

It was not, of course, easy for him to do it. When he did, he got more criticism than a white player would.

For example, in a 1949 spring

training game between the Dodgers and one of their minor league teams, some of the minor league players made fun of Jackie when he made an error. The next inning when Jackie batted he hit a single. As he ran to first base, he shouted at the minor league pitcher that he was no good. The next time Jackie batted, the minor league pitcher threw the ball near Jackie's head. He had to duck to keep from getting hit. Jackie told the pitcher that if he had hit him, he would have punched him. Later that day, the pitcher and Jackie met and shook hands to make peace.

At the same time, Jackie told reporters that other teams should expect a different sort of response from him that year. He said that he would stand up for himself and his teammates.

The commissioner of major league baseball called Jackie in for a meeting to tell him that he needed to be careful of his behavior and language. Jackie told him that he would not use violence against other teams. He only meant that he would act like any other major league player would act.

The commissioner said, "That's what I wanted to hear. You've been swell and I want you to keep up your good behavior."

As a sign that there was still a double standard, the minor league player was not called in for a meeting with the commissioner. The press talked less about the minor league player's reaction than they did Jackie's.

Even so, Jackie feeling he could be himself helped his play on the field.

That year was his greatest season.

He had a slow start. Yes, he had three hits in five times at bat on opening day. One of those hits was a home run. Then he fell into a slump. From April 20 until the end of the month, he had only six hits in forty-three at bats. His average on April 30 was .188. It was the worst average on his team.

One writer said, "Everybody can't understand how the bat that was so hot should cool off so quickly."

Another writer said that Jackie seemed like a shadow of himself.

The team was having a hard time,

too. They were in fourth place of the eight teams in the league. Jackie joked that his bad playing made it almost like he wasn't there. "When I join this club, we'll look much stronger."

When the calendar turned over to May, he began hitting. By the middle of that month, his average was .284. Then from May 15 to May 30, he had thirty-one hits in sixty-six at bats. His average jumped to .360. By the end of June, his average was .365. It was the highest in the league.

His great play helped him to break another color line in baseball.

Every summer, Major League Baseball holds an All-Star game in which the best players from the National League face the best players from the

American League. Until 1949, only white players had appeared in the game. But that year, four African Americans were All-Stars. Three came from the Brooklyn Dodgers. Besides Jackie and Campanella, there was pitcher Don Newcombe.

The fourth black player came from the American League. This was Larry Doby of the Cleveland Indians.

One more thing made this All-Star game even more historic. That year fans across the country voted for the players they thought should be All-Stars. Jackie got more votes than any other player in his league.

In the game, Jackie played well. He had one hit and a walk and he scored three runs. When it was over, he said it was a thrill to be able to play in it.

The rest of the season was good for the most part. Jackie did injure his heel in a game in August and his batting average did go down. But he hit so well before then that he still won the batting title as the best hitter in the league. He led the league in stolen bases.

His team won the National League title for the second time in Jackie's three seasons. Some said that they won it mainly because of Jackie's play. Enos Slaughter, an eventual Hall of Famer, said that "without Robinson, they would finish in the second division."

What makes this even more significant is that some stories said that

Slaughter was one of the St. Louis Cardinals who said they would strike if Jackie was on the field.

As in 1947, the Dodgers again lost the World Series to the Yankees.

Even though that was disappointing, Jackie did have another moment of glory when the season ended.

The voters who decide who receives the Most Valuable Player Award chose him as the best player in the National League.

Jackie expressed surprise that he won.

"I hardly know what to say," he told a newspaper reporter. "I really didn't expect it." He named two other players he thought should have won the award but added, "I'm tickled to death."

9.

Hall of Fame

Jackie Robinson played major league baseball until 1956. He did not win another batting title. But he was one of the best hitters in the National League over those years. He finished his career with a .311 average. This ranks as the ninety-fourth best average of all time. If ninety-fourth does not sound impressive, remember that almost 20,000 men have played major league baseball in its history.

During his career, Jackie was an All-Star for five more seasons. His team won the National League pennant four more times. In three of those years, they again lost the World Series to the New York Yankees. But in 1955, they finally managed to win the Series. That was the first Series championship in the team's history.

In his autobiography, Jackie wrote, "It was one of the greatest thrills of my life to be finally on a World Series winner."

By that time, he was thirty-six and not playing nearly as well as in his prime. That year, his batting average was .256. The next year, he was no longer in the team's regular lineup but spent many games on the bench as a substitute.

After 1956, the Dodgers decided to trade Jackie to the New York Giants. Jackie did not want to go. He retired from the game and went to work as a vice president for a restaurant chain.

Years later he told a reporter, "I gave baseball all I had for ten years and baseball has given me everything I've got today. Because of baseball, I have a wonderful position. I'm able to earn a good living for my family.

"It's a funny thing, but I never intended to play baseball, not even in the Negro Leagues. When I graduated from college, I didn't know what I was going to do. I didn't want to play baseball because of the conditions I knew I'd have to endure. I had hopes of becoming a high school coach. The only way I could become one was to get a reputation[,] so I decided to play baseball for one year."

Even though he finished playing, there was still one more honor waiting for him.

In 1962, Jackie became eligible for the Baseball Hall of Fame. For a former major league player to be admitted to the Hall of Fame, he had to have played in the big leagues for at least ten years. He had to be retired for at least five years. If a player met these rules, his name would appear on a ballot sent to the members of the Baseball Writers of America. To be elected, a player needed votes from at least seventy-five percent of the members.

When his time came, Jackie thought he would not be voted into the Hall of Fame. He thought this because there was still a lot of bias in the country against African Americans. There were still many states where African Americans could not eat in the same restaurants as white people. Even though the Supreme Court of the United States had decided in 1954 that African American students could not be barred from certain schools because of their race, there were still cities where people fought against that.

Jackie thought that he would not be elected because after he started speaking his mind in 1949, many baseball writers did not like his honesty.

As it turned out, the writers did vote Jackie in. He received seventy-seven percent of the votes.

Jackie Robinson lived for ten more years after that. Once he left the restaurant chain, he worked as an executive for an insurance company and then for a bank. For some years, he wrote a newspaper column. It was not about baseball but about politics. His column came from his work in the civil rights movement of the 1960s, trying to gain greater rights for African Americans. He once said, "I want to make sure that my children will have an equal chance. It is their future that I am concerned about."

Jackie Robinson died in 1972. On the day after his death, hundreds of newspapers across the country reported it. They praised him not only for his baseball talent but for other aspects of his life. During his career his honesty got him into trouble, but twenty-five years after he broke baseball's color line that was one of the parts of his character that newspapers praised the most.

By then, there was no longer any question whether African Americans could play baseball. Some of the game's greatest stars were those who could not have played before Jackie smashed the color line.

On April 15, 1997 Major League Baseball marked the half-century anniversary of Jackie playing the game that broke the color line. The MLB announced they would honor him by retiring the number he had worn on his jersey, forty-two. This is an honor that teams give to their greatest players but Jackie is the only player who has had his number retired by every team.

On one day of the year, the number comes out of retirement.

On April 15 every baseball season, every player on every team that takes the field that day wears number forty-two to remind people of what Jackie did and what he had to endure.

SOURCES

For this book, I turned to many sources. Some details come from several books. The three main ones were:

- *I Never Had It Made,* by Jackie Robinson with Alfred Duckett
- *Jackie Robinson,* by Arnold Rampersad
- *Only the Ball was White,* by Robert Peterson

I also found information and quotes from newspapers across the country. The main ones I used were:

- *Atlanta Constitution*
- *Brooklyn Daily Eagle*
- *Los Angeles Times*

SOURCES

- *New York Times*
- *Sporting News*
- *Washington Post*

9 781936 846719